quick & easy healthy eating

quick & easy
healthy eating

KYLE BOOKS

This edition published in 2004 by Kyle Books,
an imprint of Kyle Cathie Limited.
general.enquiries@kyle-cathie.com
www.kylecathie.com

Distributed by National Book Network
4501 Forbes Blvd., Suite 200
Lanham, MD 20706
Phone: (301) 459 3366
Fax: (301) 429 5746

ISBN 1-904920-08-X

Text © see page 176
Photographs © see page 176

The Library of Congress Cataloguing-in-Publication
Data is available on file.

Printed and bound in China by C & C Offset
Printing Co., Ltd.

contents

introduction 6

tips & shortcuts 10

better breakfasts 12

light lunches 28

delicious dinners 62

salads, soups, &

side dishes 112

delicious desserts 158

index 172

introduction

How many of us want to improve our diets but think we just haven't got the time? This book will show you that it's perfectly possible to have a healthy diet without having to spend hours in the supermarket or the kitchen. All the recipes in this book take less than 45 minutes to prepare and cook, and most of them take less than half an hour. That's less time than it takes a takeaway to arrive, and is much better for you!

constructing a healthy diet

We are bombarded every day with messages about food. On the one hand, advertisements for convenience foods, fast food restaurants, and confectionery. On the other, we hear about the latest health scare, or the latest superfoods. It can be difficult to see the wood for the trees, but the underlying principles of healthy eating haven't really changed for many years. Government guidelines suggest that a normal healthy diet consists of one third starchy foods, one third fruit and vegetables, with the other third made up of meat, fish or vegetarian alternatives, dairy products and sugars and fats. Most of us could do with cutting down on fats and sugars and increasing our intake of starchy wholegrain foods.

five a day

All of us should be aiming to eat at least 5 portions of fruit and vegetables per day. A portion counts as a slice of melon, an apple, or half a grapefruit, 3 tablespoons of cooked vegetables such as peas, sweetcorn, or carrots, or a cereal-bowl of salad. The health-giving benefits of increasing fruit and vegetable consumption are generally recognized. It is estimated that 5 portions of fruit and vegetables per day could reduce the risk of deaths from heart disease, stroke, and cancer by up to 20 percent in the population as whole.

Sometimes it may seem difficult to incorporate 5 portions of fruit and vegetables in our diet, but it is not just fresh fruit and vegetables that are important. A glass of pure fruit juice counts as a portion, as does a tablespoon of raisins, or 3 dried apricots. Frozen vegetables are as good, if not better, than some fresh vegetables as many of them are frozen immediately after picking – conserving valuable nutrients that can be depleted after a lengthy stay in a warehouse, or on the supermarket shelves.

All fruit and vegetables contain Vitamins A, C, and E, but some are richer sources than others. As a general rule, the darker or brighter the color of the vegetable the better – dark green, deep red, purple, yellow and bright orange fruit and vegetables normally have the highest levels of vitamins and minerals. Broccoli, carrots, spinach, oranges and peppers are just a few of the most vitamin-packed fruits and vegetables. Concentrate on adding colour to your shopping basket and you will automatically increase your consumption of vital nutrients.

Variety is also important. Research is still being done on the way combinations of food react in the body to provide us with their nutrients but we do know that eating a wide variety of foods, especially fruit and vegetables, increases our chances of consuming all the vitamins and minerals we need. And the more variety we eat the more we are likely to enjoy our food rather than getting bored with eating the same thing day after day.

tips & shortcuts

healthy cooking

One of the simplest ways of reducing the fat content of your food is simply to measure it. Instead of glugging a pool of oil into the skillet, measure out a tablespoon and pour that in. Use a non-stick skillet and you will not need any oil at all for some fried foods. You may be surprised at how a little oil can go a long way. In the same way you can cut down on salad dressing by measuring a tablespoonful and pouring it over your salad. Use the salad dressing to coat the salad rather than to drown it. Another good way to enjoy the taste of fried food while cutting down on the fat is to use a ridged broiler pan. Heat the pan and use a cook's brush to brush the food with a small amount of oil. When the pan is hot, place the food on the pan and cook on both sides. Any fat that comes off the meat will drain away into the ridges of the pan.

box schemes

If there is an organic vegetable box service operating in your area, you might consider joining it. This will cut down on shopping time but will also present you with a range of unusual vegetables which you may not often buy. Variety is important in the consumption of fruit and vegetables, so it can force you to be creative in order to use up all your vegetables before the next box of surprises arrives.

use your freezer

Take advantage of the wide range of frozen produce available but don't buy lots of frozen ready-meals; stock up instead on frozen vegetables which you can whip out and add to any meal. There's a lot more out there these days than just frozen peas. Add mixed frozen vegetables to a Spanish omelet or add green beans and sweetcorn to a plain frozen pizza, or just use them as easy accompaniment to any meal.

how to use this book

Each recipe provides information about the number of servings it provides, and how long it takes to prepare and cook. As a general principle, the preparation time is the time it takes to wash, prepare, and chop the ingredients for the recipe, and the cooking time is the time you actually need to spend cooking, although for much of this time the dish may be able to be left to its own devices while you get on with something else.

In addition, each recipe provides nutritional information. As a rough guide, children, sedentary women, and older adults need approximately 1,600 calories per day. Teenage girls, active women, and sedentary men need 2,200 calories, and teenage boys, active men, and very active women need up to 2,800 per day. Current advice is that no more than 10-30 percent of our daily energy intake should come from fats. Most of us should be trying to cut down on total fats, and particularly saturated fats.

Carbohydrates are an important part of everyone's diet. It is recommended that at least a third of our daily intake is made up of starchy foods such as potatoes, yams, wholegrain bread, pasta, noodles, chapattis, rice, sweet potatoes and so on.

It is recommended that our daily salt intake not exceed 6g. Most of us consume more like 9g (the equivalent of 2 teaspoonfuls). Much of the salt we consume comes from processed convenience foods, but approximately 10 percent of it comes from salt we add to our food, either during cooking or at the table. High salt consumption is implicated in raised blood pressure, which in turn has been linked to a higher risk of heart disease and stroke. There is evidence that the fiber contained in wholegrain foods and in fruit and vegetables may protect against developing some forms of heart disease and cancer.

better
breakfasts

orange & pineapple smoothie

$1/3$ cup freshly squeezed orange juice

$1/3$ cup pineapple juice

2 dessertspoons honey

8 ice cubes

juice of $1/2$ lemon

Place all ingredients in a blender, blend well and serve immediately.

TIP

This smoothie is particularly high in Vitamin C.

Nutritional value per serving:

Calories: 125

Fats: 0g

Carbohydrates: 32g

Salt: 0.03g

Saturated fat: 0g

Fiber: 0.1g

strawberry & raspberry smoothie

10 raspberries

6 strawberries

1 banana

juice of 1 orange

10 ice cubes

Blend well in a blender and serve immediately.

TIP

This smoothie is particularly high in Vitamin C.

Nutritional value per serving:

Calories: 144

Fats: 0g

Carbohydrates: 34g

Salt: 0.02g

Saturated fat: 0.1g

Fiber: 3g

fruit-filled melon shells

6oz of mixed strawberries, blueberries,
    blackberries and redcurrants
1 ripe cantaloupe melon, halved and deseeded

Wash the berries carefully, removing any hulls.

Wash the currants and strip them from their stalks, but don't bother to hull them – you'll still be there at lunchtime.

Heap the soft fruit into the hollows in the melon and serve.

TIP

This breakfast is high in Vitamins A and C.

Nutritional value per serving:
Calories: 68
Fats: 0g
Carbohydrates: 14g
Salt: 0.08g
Saturated fat: 0g
Fiber: 4.2g

compote of dried fruit

12oz mixed dried fruits – prunes, apricots,
   mangos, raisins, blueberries, apples, bananas,
   or any other that take your fancy
1$1/4$ cup plain bio-yogurt, preferably organic
2 tablespoons flax seeds

Put the fruit in a large bowl and cover with boiling water. Allow to cool, then put into the fridge overnight.

In the morning, drain the fruit. Arrange the fruit and yogurt on two plates and sprinkle the flax seeds on top.

TIP

This breakfast is particularly high in iron, calcium, and fiber.

Nutritional value per serving:

Calories: 533

Fats: 9g

Carbohydrates: 105g

Salt: 0.52g

Saturated fat: 3.5g

Fiber: 12.1g

honey, fruit, & yogurt

2 bananas, peeled and sliced

$^2/_3$ cup raspberries

1$^1/_4$ cup plain organic bio-yogurt

2 tablespoons honey, preferably organic

Divide the banana slices between 2 bowls.

Gently wash the raspberries, taking care not to bruise them, and pile on top of the bananas.

Tip half the yogurt on top of each bowl.

Drizzle with the honey.

TIP

This breakfast is particularly high in calcium and Vitamin C.

Nutritional value per serving:

Calories: 271

Fats: 6g

Carbohydrates: 48g

Salt: 0.39g

Saturated fat: 2.9g

Fiber: 3g

oatmeal porridge

1¹/₂ cups oatmeal
4 cups water
1 level teaspoon salt
light cream or milk, to serve
soft brown sugar, to serve

Bring the water to a boil and sprinkle in the oatmeal gradually, stirring all the time. Put over a low heat and stir until the water comes back to a boil. Cover and simmer for 15-20 minutes, stirring occasionally.

Add the salt and stir again. Serve with light cream or milk and soft brown sugar melting over the top.

TIP
Leftover porridge can be stored in a covered container in the fridge – it will reheat perfectly the next day.

Nutritional value per serving:
Calories: 160
Fats: 3g
Carbohydrates: 29g
Salt: 1.3g
Saturated fat: 0.7g
Fiber: 2.7g

granola

4 tablespoons rolled oats

3 tablespoons water

2 large dessert apples

1 teaspoon honey

Measure out the water into a bowl and sprinkle the oatmeal on top. Let the oatmeal soak up the water while you grate the apples, using the largest side to grate the apple coarsely, skin and all. Pick out the pips.

Stir the honey into the oatmeal and then stir in the grated apple. Taste; if it needs a little more honey add it; this depends on how much you heaped up on the spoon earlier on.

Divide it between 2 bowls. Have one yourself and give the other to your favorite person that morning. It tastes delicious just like that but will taste even better if you sprinkle over a little soft brown Barbados sugar and a little light cream.

TIP

Granola is a good source of fiber.

Nutritional value per serving:

Calories: 140

Fats: 2g

Carbohydrates: 29g

Salt: 0.01g

Saturated fat: 0.3g

Fiber: 4.6g

light
lunches

tomato, mozzarella, & avocado salad

6oz mixed dried fruits – dates, stoneless prunes, apricots, raisins, etc. – cut into raisin-sized pieces

1 quantity standard French dressing (see below)

2½ cups (12oz) fresh, young mozzarella cheese, drained and sliced

4 large tomatoes, sliced

2 kiwi fruit, peeled and sliced

2 avocados, peeled, pitted, and sliced lengthways

Soak all the fruits in freshly boiled water for 5 minutes. Drain thoroughly and stir into the dressing.

Arrange the slices of tomato, mozzarella, kiwi fruit, and avocado, in that order, on 4 plates.

Pour the French dressing over the top.

TIP

A good source of calcium, Vitamins A, B6, C, and E, as well as fiber.

To make enough French dressing to dress a salad for 4 people, place 6 tablespoons of extra-virgin olive oil, 2 tablespoons of white wine vinegar, salt, and freshly-ground pepper in a screw-top jar and shake to combine thoroughly. Dress the salad just before serving.

Nutritional value per serving:

Calories: 655

Fats: 49g

Carbohydrates: 30g

Salt: 1.67g

Saturated fat: 15.9g

Fiber: 5.4g

pickled **herring** with potato & tomato salad

12 small new potatoes

4 rollmop herrings

4oz semi sun-dried tomatoes, cubed

4 tablespoons extra-virgin olive oil

Scrub the potatoes, but don't peel them. Place in a saucepan of water, bring to a boil and cook until just tender. Leave to cool slightly.

Unwrap the rollmops, keeping all the onion inside, and place each one on a plate.

Quarter the potatoes and mix with the tomatoes. Drizzle with the olive oil.

Serve the potato and tomato mixture alongside the herrings.

Nutritional value per serving:

Calories: 378

Fats: 21g

Carbohydrates: 29g

Salt: 2.62g

Saturated fat: 3.2g

Fiber: 0.9g

shrimp, potato, & basil salad

12-16 new potatoes, diced
2 tablespoons basil leaves, torn into pieces
4 small radishes, sliced
1 scallion, chopped
juice of $\frac{1}{2}$ lime
$\frac{1}{2}$ cup plain yogurt
2 cups peeled shrimp
salt and freshly-ground black pepper
a few lettuce leaves, to serve

Boil the potatoes until tender, drain, and leave to cool. Place in a bowl with the basil, radishes, scallion, lime juice, and yogurt and mix well. Season to taste. Just before serving, gently mix in the shrimp. Arrange a few lettuce leaves on each plate and place the prawn salad on top. Serve immediately.

TIP

This salad is rich in calcium, and Vitamins B6 and C.

Nutritional value per serving:
Calories: 316
Fats: 3g
Carbohydrates: 42g
Salt: 5.26g
Saturated fat: 0.7g
Fiber: 2.5g

cypriot salad

$^1/_3$ cup haloumi cheese, cut into $^1/_4$in slices

4 medium tomatoes

$^1/_4$ cucumber, sliced

$^1/_4$ yellow bell pepper, cored, pitted, and diced

1 handful of flat-leaf parsley, roughly chopped

10 black olives, pitted

$^1/_2$ red onion, thinly sliced

3-4 large lettuce leaves, torn into pieces

Dressing

2 tablespoons extra-virgin olive oil

1 tablespoon white wine vinegar

1-2 teaspoons lemon juice

sea salt and freshly-ground black pepper

Toast the cheese under a medium broiler on a non-stick baking sheet until golden brown. Turn once and brown the other side. Mix with the other ingredients in a large salad bowl. Shake all the dressing ingredients together in a glass jar until well combined. Pour over the salad, gently toss to mix, and serve immediately.

TIP

Haloumi is available in many Mediterranean delicatessens. If you can't get hold of it, you can substitute feta.

This salad is high in Vitamins A, C, and E.

Nutritional value per serving:

Calories: 251

Fats: 20g

Carbohydrates: 11g

Salt: 2.33g

Saturated fat: 5.6g

Fiber: 3.8g

beetroot, arugula, **apple,** & cashew nut salad

1 large or 2 small fresh beetroot, peeled
   and grated
1 dessert apple, grated
1 cup fresh arugula, washed and chopped
2 tablespoons cashew nuts, chopped
1 carrot, peeled

Dressing
1 dessertspoon extra-virgin olive oil
3 dessertspoons fresh lemon juice
sea salt and freshly-ground black pepper

Place the beetroot, apple, and arugula in a salad bowl.

Place the cashew nuts on a baking sheet under the broiler on medium heat, and toast until golden brown. Turn once or twice to brown all sides. With a vegetable peeler, cut thick shavings off the peeled carrot. Add the shavings to the bowl with the cashew nuts and mix well.

Make the dressing by shaking all the ingredients together in a glass jar until well mixed. Pour over the salad and toss gently to coat. Serve immediately.

TIP

This salad is rich in folic acid and Vitamins A and C.

Nutritional value per serving:
Calories: 176
Fats: 11g
Carbohydrates: 17g
Salt: 0.61g
Saturated fat: 1.31g
Fiber: 3.5g

salad with tuna-stuffed bell pepper

2 large yellow bell peppers

$6^1/_2$oz can of tuna in olive oil, drained

1 tablespoon rinsed, chopped capers

3-4 tablespoons mayonnaise (preferably home-made)

7oz bag of mixed salad leaves

6 tablespoons French dressing (see page 30)

Preheat the oven to 350°F. Arrange the bell peppers on a baking sheet. Roast for 8-10 minutes until the skins are slightly blistered and the peppers are tender, but still holding their shape.

Transfer the peppers to a large bowl, cover with plastic wrap and leave to cool completely - this will help steam the skins off. Carefully peel away the skins, then cut each pepper in half and remove the stalks and inner membrane.

Finely chop the tuna, then transfer to a bowl, and add the capers and season to taste. Mix in enough of the mayonnaise to bind and then fill the pepper halves – this will also help them to keep their shape.

Place the salad leaves in a bowl, season, and pour in half of the dressing, tossing to coat. Arrange on serving plates and place a stuffed pepper on top of each one. Drizzle the remaining dressing over the stuffed pepper halves and serve immediately.

TIP

A good source of Vitamins B6, C, and E.

Nutritional value per serving:

Calories: 338

Fats: 30g

Carbohydrates: 6g

Salt: 1.15g

Saturated fat: 4.4g

Fiber: 2.1g

stir-fried vegetables with shrimp

1 tablespoon light soy sauce

1 tablespoon sherry vinegar

$1/2$ teaspoon Tabasco sauce

1 tablespoon sesame oil

1 teaspoon runny honey

2 tablespoons rapeseed oil – preferably organic, but certainly GM-free

2 carrots, finely sliced

4oz oyster mushrooms, sliced

1 head broccoli, cut into uniform-sized florets

2 heads pak choi, cut into 8 lengthways

$1/2$in fresh gingerroot, peeled and grated

5 fat scallions, quartered lengthways

2 cups snow peas, cut into $3/4$in pieces

8 raw king shrimp in their shells

1lb fresh beansprouts

4 tablespoons sesame seeds

Whisk together the soy sauce, sherry vinegar, Tabasco sauce, sesame oil, and runny honey and set aside.

Heat the rapeseed oil in a wok or large, deep-sided skillet. Add the carrots, mushrooms, broccoli, pak choi and gingerroot and stir-fry, stirring continuously, for 3 minutes. Add the scallions and snow peas and continue cooking for 1 minute.

Tip in the shrimp and cook for 4 minutes, until they start to change color. Tip in the beansprouts and cook for 1 minute. Add the soy sauce mixture and 3 tablespoons water and cook gently until the vegetables are tender – about 4 minutes.

Meanwhile, dry-fry the sesame seeds in a separate pan.

Serve the stir-fry with the sesame seeds scattered on top.

TIP

This dish is packed full of goodness - as well as iron, fiber, calcium, and folic acid, it also has good doses of Vitamins A, B6, C, and E.

Nutritional value per serving:

Calories: 307

Fats: 19g

Carbohydrates: 14g

Salt: 1.23g

Saturated fat: 2.1g

Fiber: 7g

crab & asparagus salad

12 asparagus spears, peeled and well trimmed

2 heads of endive

2 avocados, peeled, pitted, and sliced

2 carrots, cut into matchsticks

2¼ cups fresh white crabmeat

salt and freshly-ground black pepper

Parmesan shavings, to garnish

Lemon, mustard & Parmesan vinaigrette

1 tablespoon Dijon mustard

1 small egg yolk

1 tablespoon lemon juice

finely grated rind of ½ lemon

1 tablespoon Champagne vinegar or white
  wine vinegar

5 tablespoons extra-virgin olive oil

1½ tablespoons freshly grated Parmesan

Cook the asparagus spears in boiling salted water for 3-4 minutes or until just tender. Drain and refresh in cold water, then dry them thoroughly and cut lengthways in half.

For the dressing, whisk together the mustard, egg yolk, lemon juice and rind and vinegar, then whisk in the olive oil. Add the grated Parmesan cheese and season to taste.

Pull the leaves from the endive, wash and dry them and arrange in a salad bowl or on serving plates. Put the asparagus, avocado, carrots, and crabmeat in a separate bowl and toss gently with the dressing, then adjust the seasoning. Scatter this mixture over the endive leaves, sprinkle some coarsely cracked black pepper over the top and then scatter with the Parmesan shavings. Serve immediately.

TIP

Vegetarians can easily omit the crabmeat and replace it with more vegetables. Globe artichoke hearts, for example, would go rather well.

TIP

A nutrient-rich salad containing zinc, folic acid, fiber as well as Vitamins A, B6, C, and E.

Nutritional value per serving:

Calories: 452

Fats: 37g

Carbohydrates: 8g

Salt: 1.59g

Saturated fat: 6g

Fiber: 5.2g

spiced indian crab

1 tablespoon unscented vegetable oil

1 medium onion, finely chopped

2 garlic cloves, finely chopped

3 teaspoon medium-hot curry powder

$1/2$ teaspoon brown mustard seeds

1 teaspoon ground cumin

$1/2$ teaspoon chili powder

2 tablespoons chicken broth

3 cups picked white crabmeat, shelled

$1/4$ cup washed and dried cilantro leaves

juice of 2 lemons

salt and freshly-ground black pepper

To garnish

4 tablespoons yogurt

30 cilantro leaves, picked, washed and dried

Heat the oil in a saucepan, add the onion and garlic, and cook until soft, without browning. Add the spices and cook for a further 2-3 minutes, then pour in the broth and cook on a low heat for 10 minutes.

In a bowl mix the crabmeat, cilantro and lemon juice into the spice mixture. Season with salt and pepper.

To serve on spoons, lay teaspoons on a tray. Use a spare teaspoon to mold the crab paste on to each teaspoon. To serve, top each with a little yogurt and a cilantro leaf.

TIP

You can serve this on spoons as a canapé or use it as an excellent sandwich filling or topping for a baked potato.

This dish contains good quantities of iron and zinc.

Nutritional value per serving:

Calories: 212

Fats: 10g

Carbohydrates: 6g

Salt: 1.57g

Saturated fat: 1.3g

Fiber: 1.4g

lobster & mango salad

selection of salad leaves e.g. lollo rosso,
    butterhead, iceberg, arugula, watercress
1 ripe mango
12oz lobster tail and claw meat – a 2-2$\frac{1}{2}$lb
    lobster should yield this quantity
sprigs of chervil and borage flowers, to garnish

Dressing
6 tablespoons extra-virgin olive oil
2 tablespoons lemon juice, freshly squeezed
salt and freshly-ground pepper
pinch of sugar
2 teaspoons parsley, freshly chopped

Wash and dry the salad leaves. Combine all the ingredients for the dressing. Peel the mango and cut into slices or dice depending on presentation; sprinkle with lemon juice.

To assemble: toss the salad leaves in just enough dressing to make the leaves glisten. Arrange a little mound on each plate.

Nutritional value per serving:

Calories: 201

Fats: 12g

Carbohydrates: 10g

Salt: 0.66g

Saturated fat: 1.7g

Fiber: 1.9g

tropical salad

small bunch of cilantro
1 mango
1 papaya
14oz can of palm-hearts, drained
1½ cups small peeled shrimp, plus 12 large
   peeled shrimp, to garnish
a small bunch of scallions, thinly sliced
lime halves, to garnish

Dressing
grated rind and juice of 1 lime
1 tablespoon soy sauce
½ fresh red chile, pitted, and finely chopped
1 garlic clove, finely chopped
1 teaspoon freshly grated gingerroot
3 tablespoons vegetable oil
pulp from 1 passion fruit
½ teaspoon sugar

Remove the stalks from the cilantro, discard any woody sections and chop the stalks finely for the dressing.

Make the dressing: in a bowl, mix all the ingredients with the finely chopped cilantro stalks. Chill in the fridge while you prepare the salad.

To make the salad: first peel the mango and cut it into slices around the central pit. Cut the papaya into quarters, scoop out the seeds, then cut the papaya away from the skin, as you would a melon. Add the pieces of fruit to a bowl. Cut the palm-hearts into bite-sized pieces and add them to the fruit. Add the small shrimp to the bowl, then stir in the cilantro leaves and scallion. Pour over the dressing and toss the salad.

Pour into a serving dish, scatter the large shrimp over the top and garnish with lime halves.

TIP

This salad contains fiber, along with Vitamins A and C.

Nutritional value per serving:
Calories: 297
Fats: 10g
Carbohydrates: 25g
Salt: 5.26g
Saturated fat: 1.2g
Fiber: 5.5g

SERVES 8

PREPARATION TIME: 10 MINUTES

COOKING TIME: 20 MINUTES

spicy shrimp cous cous

$^3/_4$ cup raisins

2 cups couscous

1$^3/_4$ cups vegetable broth

2 cups cooked, peeled shrimp

$^1/_2$ large cucumber, peeled, pitted and cubed

1 red bell pepper, pitted and cubed

1 green bell pepper, deseeded and cubed

4 large plum tomatoes, pitted and roughly
  chopped

4 scallions, finely chopped

1 large carrot, grated

1 fine-skinned zucchini, grated

Dressing

$^1/_2$ cup olive oil

$^1/_2$ cup walnut oil

2 small red chiles, pitted and finely chopped

3 large scallions, trimmed and finely sliced

1 garlic clove, chopped

1in fresh gingerroot, peeled and grated

Mix all the ingredients for the dressing together in a screw-top jar and shake to combine.

Put the raisins into freshly boiled water for 1 minute. Drain.

Add the raisins to the cous cous and cook according to packet instructions – this usually takes about 20 minutes – using broth instead of water.

Add the shrimp and raw vegetables while the cous cous is still hot. Pour on the dressing and stir to mix.

Serve while still warm, or cover with plastic wrap and leave in the fridge. Bring back to room temperature before serving.

TIP

This lunch provides good amounts of iron, calcium, and Vitamins A, B6, C, and E.

Nutritional value per serving:

Calories: 480

Fats: 30g

Carbohydrates: 40g

Salt: 3g

Saturated fat: 3.5g

Fiber: 2.5g

spicy noodles with tomatoes

1½ cups egg noodles, cooked

3 tablespoons sunflower oil

½ teaspoon cumin seeds

5 garlic cloves, finely chopped

1 green chile, finely chopped

1 teaspoon freshly shredded gingerroot

good pinch ground asafetida, optional

¼ teaspoon ground turmeric

¼-½ teaspoon cayenne pepper

6 ripe tomatoes, peeled and coarsely chopped

1 medium onion, finely chopped

salt, freshly-ground pepper and sugar

3 tablespoons fresh cilantro leaves,
   finely chopped

Cook the noodles according to the instructions on the packet. Drain and reserve. Heat the oil in a wok or large, preferably non-stick frying skillet over a medium-high heat.

When hot, add the cumin seeds, stir for a few seconds. Add the garlic, chile and gingerroot. Stir and fry for 2-3 minutes until the garlic begins to color. Add the asafetida, if using, turmeric, and cayenne pepper. Stir very quickly and then, add the onions and cook for 3 or 4 minutes on a medium heat. Then toss in the chopped tomatoes, season with salt, pepper, and sugar and cook for 5-6 minutes stirring frequently. Add the cilantro, taste, and correct seasoning.

Simmer for 2-3 minutes or until the tomatoes are tender. Stir the noodles into the tomato mixture. Bubble for a minute or two to heat the noodles through. Serve immediately with lots of fresh cilantro.

TIP

There's plenty of Vitamins C and E in this dish.

Nutritional value per serving:

Calories: 228

Fats: 11g

Carbohydrates: 28g

Salt: 0.41g

Saturated fat: 1.3g

Fiber: 1.9g

green & red pasta salad

5 cups mixed tomato and spinach fusilli pasta

florets of 1 large head broccoli, very large ones
halved

4 cups baby spinach

1 red onion, very finely chopped

1¼ cups seedless black grapes, halved

½ cup extra-virgin olive oil

3 tablespoons freshly grated Parmesan cheese

Cook the pasta according to the packet instructions. Drain and put into a large, warm bowl. Meanwhile, plunge the broccoli into a saucepan of fast boiling water for 5 minutes. Wash the spinach, leaving any water still clinging to the leaves. Place in another pan, cover, and cook until wilted – this should take 3-5 minutes, depending on the age of the leaves.

Drain the green vegetables and tip them into the pasta with the onion and grapes. Stir gently but thoroughly, being careful not to break up the broccoli florets. Pour the olive oil over the mixture, add the Parmesan, mix gently again, and serve.

Cut the onion in half from top to bottom. Peel the skin, leaving the root intact. With half an onion cut-side down, make horizontal cuts towards the root, then cut the onion lengthways. Finally cut the onion crossways into dice.

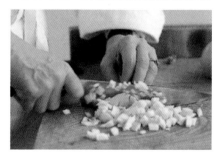

Nutritional value per serving:

Calories: 730

Fats: 34g

Carbohydrates: 89g

Salt: 0.4g

Saturated fat: 5.9g

Fiber: 7.6g

egg noodles with stir-fried vegetables

1^1/$_2$ cups noodles, dried or fresh

2 tablespoons vegetable oil

1 garlic clove, finely chopped

1 large dried red chile, roughly chopped

2 sticks celery, finely chopped

1 cup beansprouts

2 scallions, finely chopped

1 medium tomato, cut into segments

^{1}/$_2$ teaspoon chili powder

3 tablespoons light soy sauce

1 teaspoon dark soy sauce

^{1}/$_2$ teaspoon granulated sugar

Bring a saucepan of water to a boil for the noodles. If using fresh noodles, shake the strands loose, place in a strainer, and lower into the boiling water for 2-3 seconds, or until heated through. If using dried noodles, cook in the boiling water until the strands separate, by which time they will be soft. Drain and set aside.

In a wok, heat the oil until a light haze appears. Add the garlic and fry for 2-3 seconds, then add the chile and continue to stir-fry until the garlic is golden brown.

Add the cooked noodles to the pan, stir well to prevent them from sticking, then add all the remaining ingredients, stirring quickly. Turn on to a serving dish and serve.

Nutritional value per serving:

Calories: 170

Fats: 7g

Carbohydrates: 23g

Salt: 2.31g

Saturated fat: 1g

Fiber: 1.4g

chicken with peppers, guacamole, & chili oil

4 chicken breasts, skinned and each cut
   into 5 strips

chili oil

2 Romaine lettuces, large leaves torn in half

1 can Spanish red peppers, drained and halved

1 bunch cilantro

Guacamole

3 ripe avocados, peeled and stoned

juice of $\frac{1}{2}$ lemon

1 clove garlic, crushed

1 medium chile, pitted and diced

$\frac{1}{2}$ medium red onion, diced

$\frac{1}{2}$ bunch of cilantro, roughly chopped

salt and freshly-ground black pepper

To make the guacamole, mash the avocado with a fork or in a food processor. Mix in the lemon juice, garlic, chile, onion, and chopped cilantro. Season to taste.

Preheat the charbroiler or griddle pan and lightly brush the chicken with some chili oil. Place the chicken strips on the pan and grill for 5 minutes on both sides until the chicken is golden brown.

To serve, spoon some guacamole onto each plate. Top with Romaine lettuce and arrange some chicken and peppers on top. Spoon some more guacamole onto each plate and drizzle with chili oil. Serve immediately.

How to panbroil chicken breasts

Heat a ridged broiler pan. Brush each chicken breast (not the grill) with a little sesame oil, then season the chicken breasts, and place on the grill. Cook for 5-6 minutes on each side, until lightly charred and cooked through.

Nutritional value per serving:

Calories: 402

Fats: 24g

Carbohydrates: 10g

Salt: 0.61g

Saturated fat: 3.1g

Fiber: 5.8g

delicious
dinners

steamed citrus **mussels**

1 garlic clove, crushed

$1/2$in gingerroot, peeled and finely sliced

2 stems fresh lemongrass, outer leaves removed and finely chopped

4 tablespoons rice wine vinegar or white wine vinegar

50ml (2fl oz) dry white wine (optional) or water

juice of $1/2$ lemon

2lb fresh mussels, beards removed, and well scrubbed

6 tablespoons reduced-fat coconut milk

juice of 1 lime

Place the garlic, gingerroot, lemongrass, vinegar, wine, and lemon juice in a large saucepan, bring to a boil, and simmer for 5 minutes. Add the mussels to the pan, cover with a lid, and cook over a low heat for 3-4 minutes, shaking the pan occasionally. When the mussels open, add the coconut milk and the lime juice, cover and shake once or twice to coat all the mussels in the sauce. Discard any mussels which are not open and serve immediately.

TIP

There are high levels of iron and zinc in this dish.

Nutritional value per serving:

Calories: 181

Fats: 7g

Carbohydrates: 7g

Salt: 1.45g

Saturated fat: 3.8g

Fiber: 0.2g

How to debeard mussels

To remove the beards from mussels, hold the mussel with the pointed end away from you. Pull downwards on the beard to remove it. Scrub the mussels well before cooking.

scallops with gingerroot, scallion, & tamarind

1 tablespoon tamarind paste
$^3/_4$in piece of gingerroot, peeled and grated
2 scallions, thinly sliced lengthways and soaked in iced water
3 tablespoons vegetable oil, plus more for the pan
1 tablespoon toasted sesame oil
12 scallops
salt

Place the tamarind paste in a saucepan with 4 tablespoons of water and heat gently, stirring to extract as much of the tamarind as possible. Set aside and allow to cool.

Strain and combine with the grated gingerroot, drained scallions and both types of oil.

Season the scallops with salt. Get a skillet good and hot and then oil it lightly. When the oil is hot, fry the scallops over as high a heat as you can manage for no more than 45 seconds on each side.

Place the scallops on small shallow plates or, better still, in well-scrubbed scallop shells, and spoon over the tamarind mixture.

TIP

If the scallops are really thick, they will sometimes remain cold and uncooked in the middle in the time it takes the exterior to cook perfectly. You can avoid this – and make the scallops go further – by cutting them across into two rounds.

Nutritional value per serving:
Calories: 263
Fats: 18g
Carbohydrates: 3g
Salt: 0.92g
Saturated fat: 2.3g
Fiber: 0.1g

seared **scallops** with guacamole, cilantro, & chile

1 avocado
juice of 1 lemon
juice of 1 lime
1¼ cups cilantro leaves, chopped
1 clove garlic, chopped
1 chile, pitted and diced
4 tablespoons chives, chopped
1 tablespoon olive oil
2 tablespoons butter
12 fresh scallops
2 tablespoons reduced-fat coconut milk
cilantro sprigs
salt and freshly-ground black pepper

Avocado salad
1 avocado, diced
1 chile, pitted and diced
1 cup cilantro leaves, chopped

Peel and pit the avocado and dice finely. Place in a small bowl, add the lemon and lime juice and season with salt and pepper. Process the cilantro, garlic, chile and chives in a food processor, then mix in with the avocado.

Heat the olive oil and butter in a small skillet. Season the scallops then sear for 1 minute on each side. Mix the ingredients for the salad in a bowl. Serve the scallops with spoonfuls of guacamole and avocado salad.

Garnish with coconut milk and cilantro.

How to prepare scallops

With the flat side of the scallop upwards, slide a sharp knife between the two halves of the shell to cut the nerve holding them closed. Remove and discard the top shell. Slide the knife underneath the exposed scallop and ease it off the shell. Discard the black tissue around it and cut off the black vein that runs around the side of the scallop.

Nutritional value per serving:
Calories: 345
Fats: 26g
Carbohydrates: 3g
Salt: 1.14g
Saturated fat: 7.9g
Fiber: 2.7g

clams with chile & basil

1lb fresh baby clams in their shells

2 tablespoons vegetable oil

2 garlic cloves, finely chopped

1 tablespoon chili oil

2 tablespoons *nam pla* (Thai fish sauce)

2 tablespoons fish broth or water

$^1/_2$ teaspoon granulated sugar

1 long fresh red chile, finely slivered

20 fresh basil leaves, shredded

Rinse the clams under cold water, discarding any that do not close when shaken. Drain and set aside.

In a wok or skillet, heat the oil and fry the garlic until golden brown. Add the clams and chili oil and stir thoroughly. Add all the remaining ingredients in turn, stirring after each addition, and cook over a high heat until the clams open. Discard any clams that remain closed.

Pour into a serving bowl and serve.

Nutritional value per serving:

Calories: 1.5

Fats: 9g

Carbohydrates: 2g

Salt: 1.43g

Saturated fat: 1.1g

Fiber: 0.1g

fisherman's clams

4lb clams or any fresh shellfish

2 tablespoons olive oil

2 garlic cloves, finely chopped

1 green frying chile, pitted and chopped

1 fresh red chile, pitted and finely chopped

1 tablespoon chopped parsley

Pick over the clams and rinse thoroughly. Heat the oil in a roomy saucepan and fry the garlic and chiles for 2-3 minutes, just enough to perfume the oil. Tip in the shellfish, turn up the heat, and bubble for 3-4 minutes, until all the shells gape open in the steam – turn them with a spoon so that the ones on top can get to the heat. When all are open, they're done. Remove the pan from the heat immediately – shellfish toughens if it's overcooked. Finish with freshly-chopped parsley.

TIP

Leave the clams to soak overnight in cold water and discard any with cracked or gaping shells and those which feel too heavy – a sign they're full of something other than live fish. Shellfish can stay fresh for as long as they can hold water in their shells.

Nutritional value per serving:

Calories: 134

Fats: 7g

Carbohydrates: 1g

Salt: 0.19g

Saturated fat: 1g

Fiber: 0.2g

stir-fried crab claws with scallion, chili, & garlic

Chili paste

1 red chile, pitted and finely chopped

2 cloves garlic, chopped

$\frac{1}{2}$in gingerroot, peeled and chopped

$1\frac{1}{2}$ tablespoons rice wine vinegar

1 tablespoon superfine sugar

$\frac{1}{2}$ teaspoon sea salt

$\frac{1}{2}$ cup vegetable oil

1 tablespoon chili paste

4in gingerroot, peeled and sliced

4 crab claws, boiled, shell cracked, and cleaned

2 tablespoons *nam pla* (Thai fish sauce)

4 scallions, thinly sliced, green parts reserved
   for garnish

freshly-ground black pepper

cilantro leaves, to garnish

To make the chili paste: Blend the chile, garlic and gingerroot in a food processor until it forms a rough paste. Add the rice wine vinegar, sugar, and salt and mix well.

Heat the vegetable oil in a wok over a medium heat. Add the chili paste and stir-fry for 1-2 minutes. Add the gingerroot and crab claws. Stir in the fish sauce and add the scallions. Toss well, reduce the heat, and place a lid or a piece of aluminum foil on top. Cook for 2-3 minutes, shaking the wok. Season with black pepper and serve immediately, garnished with scallion strips and cilantro leaves.

Nutritional value per serving:

Calories: 662

Fats: 64g

Carbohydrates: 7g

Salt: 3.87g

Saturated fat: 7.2g

Fiber: 0.3g

squid with dry curry

6-8oz squid (bodies only), washed and cleaned

2 tablespoons vegetable oil

2 garlic cloves, finely chopped

2 teaspoons red curry paste

1 tablespoon *nam pla* (Thai fish sauce)

1 tablespoon light soy sauce

1 teaspoon granulated sugar

2-3 small green eggplants, quartered

1 small fresh red chile, finely chopped

2 kaffir lime leaves, finely sliced

10 fresh basil leaves

Score the squid finely on both sides, then cut into pieces about 1in square. Set aside. In a wok or skillet, heat the oil and fry the garlic until golden brown. Stir in the curry paste and cook for a few seconds. Add the squid, coating it in the sauce. Add the fish sauce, soy sauce, sugar and eggplants and stir-fry over a high heat until the eggplants are cooked through. Now stir in the chile, lime leaves, and basil.

When the squid is cooked through and opaque, give the dish a final stir and pour into a serving dish.

How to prepare squid

Cut off the tentacles then pull the entrails out of the sac and discard. Remove the 'beak' and pull the quill out of the sac. Pull off the wings and scrape the purplish membrane off them and the sac. Cut the body into rings.

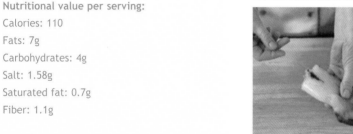

Nutritional value per serving:

Calories: 110

Fats: 7g

Carbohydrates: 4g

Salt: 1.58g

Saturated fat: 0.7g

Fiber: 1.1g

seared fillet of **salmon** with new potatoes & citrus salad

16 small new potatoes, scrubbed clean

3 oranges, segmented as shown below, juice reserved

3 lemons, segmented as shown below, juice reserved

About ¹/₂ cup olive oil

4 salmon fillets, skinned

4 tablespoons chopped fresh cilantro

2 cups arugula leaves

Boil the potatoes in salted water for 12-15 minutes until just tender. Drain, allow to cool a little, and slice. Season and drizzle over a little of the olive oil. Place the orange and lemon segments in a separate bowl. Add all except 1 tablespoon of the olive oil to the juices and whisk together to combine, then season to taste. Heat a non-stick skillet and add the remaining olive oil. Season the salmon fillets and add to the pan and cook for 3-4 minutes until seared and lightly golden. Turn over and cook for another minute until just tender. Transfer to a plate and keep warm. Tip the orange and lemon segments into the dressing and then add the cilantro and arugula leaves, tossing to combine. Arrange the salmon fillets on serving plates and place the new potatoes on the side with the arugula salad on top.

How to segment citrus fruit

Use a sharp knife to cut off the top and bottom of the fruit, then peel the skin and pith in a spiral. Cut in front of each membrane towards the centre of the fruit then push the knife forward to remove the segment cleanly. Continue all around the fruit.

Nutritional value per serving:

Calories: 644

Fats: 45g

Carbohydrates: 29g

Salt: 0.22g

Saturated fat: 7.1g

Fiber: 3.9g

medallion of **cod** with soy & choy sum

2lb choy sum (available from Asian markets),
  shredded
juice of 1 lemon
5 cloves garlic, crushed
1in gingerroot, peeled and grated
2 tablespoons sweet soy sauce
1 tablespoon olive oil
4 large (about 2lb) cod or other firm white fish
  fillets, cut into 12 medallions
1 carrot, cut into thin strips
4 scallions, cut into thin strips
$1/2$ stick butter, cubed
1 large red chile pepper, pitted and cut
  into strips
salt and freshly-ground black pepper

Blanch the choy sum in a saucepan of boiling, salted water for 3 minutes and refresh under cold water. Drain well. Rinse out the pan.

Combine the lemon juice, garlic, grated gingerroot and soy sauce in a bowl.

Place the oil in the pan over a high heat and cook the fish for 1 minute on each side. Add the choy sum, carrot, and scallions, and the garlic mixture. Increase the heat and add the butter. Swirl the pan to incorporate the butter, season well, and sprinkle with the chile strips. Serve immediately.

TIP

This dish is a good source of iron, folic acid as well as Vitamins A and C.

Nutritional value per serving:
Calories: 352
Fats: 15g
Carbohydrates: 12g
Salt: 3.31g
Saturated fat: 7.2g
Fiber: 0.9g

grilled **flounder** on the bone

4 very fresh whole flounders

salt and freshly-ground pepper

butter, for frying

$1/2$-1 stick butter

4 teaspoons mixed fresh parsley, chives, and
    thyme leaves, finely chopped

Remove the head from the fish. Score the skin crossways on both sides, sprinkle with a little salt and pepper, and spread butter on both sides of the fish. Grill for 10-12 minutes at a medium heat; you will need to turn the fish once during the cooking time, which will depend on the size or thickness of the fish. Meanwhile, melt the butter and stir in the freshly chopped herbs. Spoon the herb butter over the fish and serve immediately.

How to chop fresh herbs

Wash and dry the herbs, discarding the stalks or saving them for the brothpot. Gather the herbs into a little ball and chop roughly. Change the angle of the knife to a horizontal position and rock the blade backwards and forwards until the herbs are chopped finely.

Nutritional value per serving:

Calories: 317

Fats: 14g

Carbohydrates: 0g

Salt: 0.87g

Saturated fat: 7.2g

Fiber: 0.1g

baked **mackerel** with carrot noodles

4 large carrots

4 x 8oz mackerel

1 teaspoon coriander seeds, crushed

2 shallots, finely diced

rind of 1 orange, grated

2 tablespoons fresh cilantro leaves, finely
   chopped

1 tablespoon balsamic vinegar

2 tablespoons extra-virgin olive oil

salt and freshly-ground black pepper

Using a potato peeler, shave the carrots into noodles. Season the mackerel fillets with salt, pepper and the crushed coriander seeds. Place on a baking sheet skin-side up and bake in a pre-heated oven at 450°F for 10 minutes.

Meanwhile, bring a saucepan of salted water to a boil and blanch the carrot noodles for a couple of seconds, then refresh under cold running water and drain well.

In a bowl mix together the shallots, orange rind, cilantro leaves, vinegar, oil, and seasoning. When the fish is ready, arrange the noodles on a serving plate and season with a little of the dressing. Place the fish fillets on top, spoon over the remaining dressing and serve.

Nutritional value per serving:

Calories: 475

Fats: 34g

Carbohydrates: 9g

Salt: 0.34g

Saturated fat: 6.1g

Fiber: 2.2g

gray mullet in a parcel

6 pieces of aluminum foil measuring 8 x 8in

3 tablespoons olive oil

1 medium fennel, sliced across thinly

1 medium onion, sliced into thin rings

6 gray mullets, cleaned and washed

a few sprigs of thyme

2 cloves of garlic, sliced thinly

6 thin slices of lemon

salt and freshly-ground black pepper

lemon wedges, to serve

Preheat the oven to 400°F.

Oil the center of each aluminum foil square generously (this will use roughly half the oil) and distribute the sliced fennel and onion evenly.

Stuff the cavity of each fish with a sprig of thyme and the garlic and lay them on top of the vegetables. Sprinkle with the rest of the oil. Lay a slice of lemon on each, season with salt and pepper, and parcel up tightly. Bake in the preheated oven for 10- 15 minutes, opening the parcels for the last 5 minutes.

When the fish is nicely browned, serve decorated with lemon wedges. If more salt is needed, sprinkle with a bit of coarse sea salt.

Nutritional value per serving:

Calories: 292

Fats: 15g

Carbohydrates: 4g

Salt: 0.68g

Saturated fat: 3.2g

Fiber: 1.3g

steamed fish with chili paste

2 long dried red chiles, pitted and soaked in
    water to soften

3 garlic cloves, chopped

3 small red shallots, chopped

1in piece of galangal, peeled and coarsely
    chopped

1 tablespoon chopped lemongrass

1lb firm white fish, filleted and cut into
    1in chunks

2 tablespoons *nam pla* (Thai fish sauce)

2 fresh sweet basil leaves

Using a pestle and mortar, pound together the chiles, garlic, shallots, galangal, and lemongrass to make a paste.

Place the fish pieces in a mixing bowl with the fish sauce, basil leaves, and paste and mix gently together.

Place the mixture in a heatproof bowl and steam for 15 minutes. Serve in the bowl.

TIP

Galangal is a creamy-white rhizome and is slightly harder than ginger. It is used in the same way, but has a more lemony flavor.

Nutritional value per serving:

Calories: 89

Fats: 1g

Carbohydrates: 3g

Salt: 1.42g

Saturated fat: 0.1g

Fiber: 0.3g

grilled **tuna** with salsa verde

4 x 7oz tuna steaks
olive oil, for brushing
1 lemon, quartered, to serve

Salsa verde
1 garlic clove
bunch of flat-leaf parsley, chopped
1 scallion, finely chopped
2 anchovy fillets, finely chopped
1 teaspoon Dijon mustard
1 dessertspoon capers
4 tablespoons olive oil
salt and freshly-ground black pepper

Preheat a hot broiler.

Make the salsa verde: finely chop the garlic and crush it with a little salt. Work all the ingredients except the oil in a mortar with a pestle until they form a rough paste. Whisk in the olive oil (you may need a little more) until the sauce has a thick consistency. Adjust the seasoning.

Lightly brush the tuna with olive oil, season well with salt and pepper, and broil for 2 minutes each side.

Serve each tuna steak with a generous spoonful of the salsa and a lemon quarter.

Nutritional value per serving:
Calories: 394
Fats: 22g
Carbohydrates: 1g
Salt: 0.89g
Saturated fat: 4.8g
Fiber: 0.3g

baked stuffed **trout**

4 tablespoons extra-virgin olive oil

1 small onion, finely chopped

1 garlic clove, finely chopped

1 teaspoon paprika

1 teaspoon cayenne pepper

1 x 8oz can chopped tomatoes

1 x 7oz can garbanzo beans, drained

4 large sprigs flat-leaf parsley, finely chopped

juice of 1 large lemon

4 small salmon trout, trimmed and gutted

$2/3$ cup dry white wine

$1/2$ stick unsalted butter

salt and freshly-ground black pepper

Preheat the oven to 425°F.

Heat the oil in a skillet, add the onions and garlic, and sweat gently for 5 minutes. Stir in the paprika and cayenne pepper and cook for a further 2 minutes. Add the tomatoes and garbanzo beans and simmer until tender – about 10 minutes.

Mash the mixture roughly, pouring off any excess tomato juice until you have the consistency of a stuffing. Add the parsley and lemon juice and mix into the stuffing. Pile the stuffing into the trout cavities.

Cut 4 pieces of aluminum foil big enough to totally envelope each fish. Put each trout on a piece of foil. Divide the wine among them, season, dot with the butter and seal the parcels. Bake for 20 minutes. Open the foil carefully to let the steam escape before serving.

Nutritional value per serving:

Calories: 476

Fats: 29g

Carbohydrates: 9g

Salt: 0.55g

Saturated fat: 9.7g

Fiber: 2.1g

chicken tortillas with avocado, chili, & sour cream

14oz boneless, skinless chicken, diced

2 tablespoons olive oil

4 soft flour tortillas, each about 8in in diameter

2 ripe avocados

2 heaped tablespoons sour cream

1 ripe tomato, peeled, pitted, and diced

1 red chile, pitted and finely chopped

Preheat the broiler or a griddle pan. Thread the chicken on to soaked wooden skewers, making sure they are not too tightly packed together. Brush with the olive oil and cook for 4-5 minutes, depending on the size of the dice or until the chicken is completely tender and lightly charred. Leave until cool enough to handle.

Place the tortillas on the broiler rack and then place under the broiler for 30 seconds to 1 minute to just warm through, turning once. Alternatively, use the griddle pan.

Meanwhile, remove the chicken from the skewers. Peel the avocados and then cut each one in half and remove the pits. Cut the flesh into $\frac{1}{2}$in dice. Spread the softened tortillas with the sour cream and scatter the chicken down the center of each one. Place the avocado on top with the tomato dice and chile, then roll up to enclose the filling completely.

Return to the broiler rack and place under the broiler, seam-side down for 1-2 minutes until the tops are lightly toasted; or use the griddle pan. Cut each tortilla in half on the diagonal and arrange on warmed serving plates. Serve immediately.

Nutritional value per serving:

Calories: 480

Fats: 25g

Carbohydrates: 35g

Salt: 0.6g

Saturated fat: 5g

Fiber: 4g

TIP

Keep a packet of flour tortillas in the cupboard - they often come in handy. To make them soft enough for rolling, place them under the broiler or on a skillet or griddle pan. Alternatively, they can also be microwaved on high between dampened paper towels for about 20 seconds.

pan-broiled chicken breasts with cardamom

8 chicken breasts

1 teaspoon cardamom seeds

1 teaspoon black peppercorns

good pinch cayenne pepper

4 tablespoons olive oil

$1/2$ stick butter

finely grated rind and juice of 1 lemon

Flatten the chicken breasts slightly. Pound the cardamom and peppercorns together in a mortar and add the cayenne and olive oil. Dip the chicken breasts in this marinade, cover and leave to marinade for about 2 hours.

Pan-broil the chicken breasts or barbecue them on an oiled rack about 5in from the coals, cook for several minutes each side, brushing with extra marinade while cooking. Cream the butter, add the finely grated lemon rind, and beat in the juice very gradually.

Spoon the butter over the chicken breasts and serve with a good green salad.

Nutritional value per serving:

Calories: 249

Fats: 12g

Carbohydrates: 1g

Salt: 0.33g

Saturated fat: 4.5g

Fiber: 0g

whole boneless quail with peaches

4 whole boneless oven-ready quail

2 tablespoons light muscovado sugar

8 ripe peaches, halved and pitted

2½ cups muscat wine

2 vanilla pods, split

2 head of Swiss chard, cut into julienne as
   shown below

Preheat the oven to 400°F. Place the quails in the center of a large ovenproof dish, using cocktail sticks to help keep them in shape. Roast in the oven for 3-5 minutes until golden brown, then drizzle with olive oil and season to taste. Return to the oven and cook for another minute or two or until the juices just begin to run. Remove from the oven and sprinkle the sugar over the quails. Surround with the peaches and pour in the muscat wine. Tuck in the vanilla pods and sprinkle the Swiss chard julienne on top. Return to oven and cook for another 5-7 minutes or until the quails are completely tender. Bring the dish straight to the table and serve in warmed wide-rimmed bowls.

TIP

Boneless quail are available in most major supermarkets or you could always try and get your butcher to prepare them for you - just give some advance notice.

How to julienne Swiss chard

Wash and dry the leaves. Remove the midribs with a sharp knife. (Use them for another recipe.) Roll up each leaf tightly and cut each roll into fine slices.

Nutritional value per serving:

Calories: 526

Fats: 14g

Carbohydrates: 35g

Salt: 0.48g

Saturated fat: 3.4g

Fiber: 3.3g

vietnamese pork & lemongrass patties

2 cups lean, ground pork

1 shallot, chopped

2 stalks lemongrass, trimmed and very finely
  chopped

$1/2$ teaspoon salt

lots of freshly-ground black pepper

Put everything into a food processor, season well with salt and pepper, and whizz for just a few seconds. Heat a skillet and cook a tiny piece to check the seasoning, adjusting if necessary.

Make the meat mixture into patties up to 3in in diameter and pan-broil for 5 minutes on each side. Or you can make the meat into small balls about 2in in diameter and thread them onto well-soaked bamboo skewers and barbecue them for 10-15 minutes, turning on all sides.

Nutritional value per serving:

Calories: 143

Fats: 5g

Carbohydrates: 1g

Salt: 0.81g

Saturated fat: 1.5g

Fiber: 0.1g

calves' liver with almonds

leaves of 1 large sprig rosemary, finely chopped

2 garlic cloves, very finely chopped

1 1/2 cups fresh wholewheat breadcrumbs

1 cup ground almonds

2 pinches ground saffron

4 tablespoons extra-virgin olive oil

1/2 stick unsalted butter

4 x 6oz slices calves' liver

2/3 cup red wine

3/4 cup raisins

freshly-ground black pepper

steamed carrots and broccoli, to serve

Mix the rosemary, garlic, breadcrumbs, almonds, and saffron into half the oil. Season with black pepper.

Heat the butter and remaining oil in a large skillet. Add the liver and cook for 3-4 minutes, depending on thickness and how pink you like it, turning once. Remove and keep warm.

Put all the other ingredients into the pan and boil briskly for 2 minutes, stirring to loosen any liver stuck to the bottom.

Serve the liver with the sauce spooned over the top and accompanied by steamed carrots and broccoli.

TIP

This dish is packed with goodness - iron, zinc and folic acid as well as Vitamins A, B6, and C. Pregnant or breastfeeding women are advised to limit their consumption of liver to one portion per week.

Nutritional value per serving:

Calories: 707

Fats: 43g

Carbohydrates: 33g

Salt: 0.76g

Saturated fat: 11.3g

Fiber: 4.3g

lamb steaks with fresh apricot sauce

2 tablespoons honey

2 tablespoons olive oil

4-6 x 6oz lamb steaks

salt and freshly-ground black pepper

Apricot sauce

5-8 medium fresh apricots, kernels removed, or
   $1^3/_4$ cups dried apricots

1-2 tablespoons honey, to taste

2 tablespoons chopped mint (or 1 tablespoon
   dried)

few drops of lemon juice

$1/_2$ teaspoon grated lemon rind

salt and freshly-ground black pepper

Heat the grill to maximum. Mix the honey with the oil and brush over the steaks. Season with salt and pepper. Grill at a high heat for 4-5 minutes each side. this will result in a medium-rare lamb steak; if you like your lamb well done, grill for a few minutes more.

Put all the sauce ingredients into a food processor and process to a smooth puree.

Decorate each steak with a sprig of mint and serve on a pool of sauce.

Nutritional value per serving:

Calories: 355

Fats: 18g

Carbohydrates: 17g

Salt: 0.78g

Saturated fat: 6.7g

Fiber: 2g

marinated steak skewers

1 onion, thinly sliced

4in fresh gingerroot, peeled and cut into
   julienne

$^1/_2$ cup dark soy sauce

1lb steak, cut into 1in cubes

4 tablespoons olive oil

1$^1/_2$ cups shiitake mushrooms, sliced

2 carrots, peeled and cut into julienne, as
   shown below

Place the onion, gingerroot and soy sauce in a shallow non-metallic dish. Add the steak cubes, stirring to combine, then cover with plastic wrap and chill for at least 3 hours, or overnight is fine.

Heat a large non-stick skillet until hot. Drain the beef from the marinade, reserving it to use later, then thread the beef on to 8 x 6in wooden skewers. Add the oil to the pan and when the oil begins to smoke, sear the skewers on all sides – you may have to do this in two batches, depending on the size of your pan. Transfer to a warmed plate and keep warm.

Add the mushrooms and carrots to the same pan that you have cooked the beef in, then sauté for 2 minutes. Add four tablespoons of the reserved marinade, reduce the heat and continue to cook for about 1 minute, stirring occasionally. Arrange the skewers on warmed serving plates with the vegetables and spoon over any remaining sauce. Serve at once.

How to julienne vegetables

Wash and peel the vegetable. Square off the sides (saving the trimmings for the brothpot) and cut the vegetables crossways into 2in lengths. Cut lengthways into thin slices then stack and cut lengthways into thin strips.

Nutritional value per serving:

Calories: 313

Fats: 17g

Carbohydrates: 12g

Salt: 5.94g

Saturated fat: 3.6g

Fiber: 1.5g

SERVES 4

PREPARATION TIME: 10 MINUTES

COOKING TIME: 15 MINUTES

beef & vegetable noodles with black beans

2 tablespoons vegetable oil

3¹/₂ cups cooked egg noodles, drained and
   separated

1 tablespoon light soy sauce

1 garlic clove, finely chopped

1 x 4oz beef steak, finely sliced

1 tablespoon *nam pla* (Thai fish sauce)

4 tablespoons beef broth, plus extra if
   necessary

1 teaspoon black bean sauce

1 teaspoon all-purpose flour mixed with 4
   tablespoons water to make a thin paste (this
   will give more than you need)

4oz mixed green vegetables (young cabbage,
   snow peas, broccoli, for example)

¹/₂ teaspoon granulated sugar

¹/₄ teaspoon ground white pepper

In a wok or skillet, heat 1 tablespoon oil. Add the noodles and stir-fry quickly to prevent them from sticking. Add the soy sauce and stir-fry for 30-60 seconds. Turn on to a serving dish, keep warm and set aside.

Add the remaining oil to the wok and fry the garlic until golden brown. Add the beef and stir-fry over a high heat until the meat loses its red color. Stir in the fish sauce, a little broth and the black bean sauce. Thicken with a little of the flour and water mixture, stirring all the time to prevent lumps forming. Toss in the vegetables and sugar and stir-fry for a few seconds. Season with pepper, stir once, then pour over the noodles and serve.

Nutritional value per serving:

Calories: 140

Fats: 7g

Carbohydrates: 11g

Salt: 1.55g

Saturated fat: 1.2g

Fiber: 1.1g

okra and bean stew

4 corn on the cob, husks removed

$^1/_2$ stick unsalted butter

12-16 small okra, trimmed

4 scallions, shredded

$^1/_2$ red bell pepper, cut into small dice

$^1/_2$ green bell pepper, cut into small dice

$^1/_2$ garlic clove, crushed

$^1/_2$ teaspoon dried thyme

$^1/_2$ teaspoon ground paprika

$^1/_2$ teaspoon ground cumin

1 x 14oz can of butter beans

$1^1/_2$ teaspoons lemon juice

salt and freshly-ground black pepper

Using a small knife, shuck the corn kernels into a bowl along with any juices from the corn, as shown below.

Dice half the butter and chill it. Heat the remaining butter in a large skillet, add the okra, scallions and bell peppers and cook over a moderate heat for 3-4 minutes. Add the shucked corn, garlic, thyme, and spices, lower the heat and cook until fragrant, about 4-5 minutes. Add the canned beans and their liquid, stirring them in to heat through. Season to taste, stir in the lemon juice and then whisk in the reserved butter a few pieces at a time.

TIP

This vegetarian dish is a valuable source of iron, calcium, folic acid, and fibre, as well as Vitamins A, B6, and C. Butter beans provide low-fat protein.

How to remove corn kernels

Remove the husks and the silky threads from the corn cobs. Hold each cob upright on a work surface and cut off the kernels with a sharp knife.

Nutritional value per serving:

Calories: 275

Fats: 14g

Carbohydrates: 30g

Salt: 0.89g

Saturated fat: 6.5g

Fiber: 8.4g

salads,
soups,
& side
dishes

cabbage & beetroot soup

4 tablespoons canola oil

1 onion, finely chopped

1 garlic clove, finely chopped

12-16 raw baby beetroot, diced

2 cups vegetable broth

2 tablespoons cider vinegar

3 cups white cabbage, coarsely shredded (see page 154)

8 chives

Heat the oil in a large saucepan, add the onion and garlic, and sweat gently for 5 minutes.

Mix in the beetroot, pour in the broth and boil until tender. Whizz in a blender with the cider vinegar and return to the saucepan.

Scatter the cabbage on the soup, but don't stir. Cover and boil gently for 5 minutes, until the cabbage is almost cooked but still crunchy.

Serve with chives arranged on top.

Nutritional value per serving:

Calories: 178

Fats: 11g

Carbohydrates: 15g

Salt: 1.03g

Saturated fat: 0.8g

Fiber: 4.1g

mussel soup with fine beans, tomato, & cilantro

3lb 5oz mussels, cleaned and debearded (see page 64)

1¼ cups dry white wine

3 tablespoons olive oil

1 onion, finely chopped

1½ cups fine green beans, finely chopped

3 plum tomatoes, peeled, pitted, and diced

1 bunch of fresh cilantro, leaves stripped and chopped

white peppercorns (optional)

Prepare the mussels, discarding any that won't close when they are lightly tapped on the work surface.

Heat a large saucepan over a high heat. Tip in the mussels and cover for 10-15 seconds, then pour over the wine and 1¼ cups of water. Add a few white peppercorns if you've got them, then cover and cook, shaking the pan every now and then, for 5 minutes or until all the mussels have opened. Discard any that stay closed.

Tip the mussels into a colander set over a large bowl and then pass the cooking liquid once more through a fine strainer and reserve. When the mussels are cool enough to handle, remove the mussel meats from their shells and reserve, discarding the shells.

Heat a saucepan. Add one tablespoon of the olive oil and then add the onion. Cook for a few minutes until softened, then pour in the reserved cooking liquid and bring to a boil. Season to taste. Add the beans, mussels, and tomatoes and just warm through. Ladle into warmed wide-rimmed bowls, scatter over the cilantro and drizzle over the remaining olive oil. Serve immediately.

Nutritional value per serving:

Calories: 245

Fats: 11g

Carbohydrates: 10g

Salt: 0.86g

Saturated fat: 1.5g

Fiber: 2.4g

chilled avocado soup

5 ripe avocados, peeled and pitted

2 cups chicken broth

juice of 1 large lemon

2 large garlic cloves, finely chopped

3 red chiles, pitted and chopped

$1/4$ teaspoon cayenne pepper

4 plump scallions, roughly chopped

leaves of 12 large stems cilantro

1 x 7oz can organic plum tomatoes, drained

$2/3$ cup plain organic bio-yogurt

4 tablespoons pumpkin seeds

salt and freshly-ground black pepper

Put the avocado flesh into a food processor with the chicken broth and add the lemon juice.

Add the garlic, chiles and cayenne pepper and blend smooth.

Add the scallions, cilantro leaves, and tomatoes, and process briefly again.

Add the yogurt and whizz for just a few seconds. Adjust the seasoning and leave in the fridge to chill.

Serve decorated with pumpkin seeds.

Nutritional value per serving:

Calories: 450

Fats: 41g

Carbohydrates: 10g

Salt: 1.22g

Saturated fat: 6g

Fiber: 6.9g

spiced gazpacho

1/2 small cucumber

4 medium good quality fresh tomatoes

1/2 red onion

1/2 yellow bell pepper, cored and pitted

1 garlic clove, crushed

1 red chile, pitted and finely chopped

1 small handful parsley

1 small handful cilantro

1 dessertspoon extra-virgin olive oil

pinch of paprika

1 tablespoon cider vinegar

sea salt and freshly-ground black pepper

parsley and cilantro leaves, to garnish

Place all ingredients except the herbs for garnishing in a food processor and blend until the mixture is well chopped, but not puréed. Serve at room temperature, garnished.

Nutritional value per serving:

Calories: 115

Fats: 6g

Carbohydrates: 14g

Salt: 0.32g

Saturated fat: 0.7g

Fiber: 4.1g

chilled asparagus & lemon soup

10-12 asparagus spears, trimmed and peeled

$1/2$ cup vegetable broth or water

1 small onion, finely chopped

1 medium potato, peeled and diced

$3^1/_4$ cups water

2 tablespoons chopped oregano

juice of 1 lemon

salt and freshly-ground black pepper

lemon rind, to garnish

Cut off the tips of the asparagus and reserve. Cut the rest into thin strips $3/_4$-$1^1/_4$in long. Heat the broth in a saucepan, add the onion, cover, and simmer gently for 5 minutes. Add the potato to the pan with the asparagus strips and water, bring to a boil and simmer for 10 minutes, until the potato and asparagus are very soft. Add the oregano and lemon juice to the pan and simmer for 2-3 minutes, then blend in a blender or food processor.

Steam the asparagus tips for 2-3 minutes until just tender and add to the smooth soup. Season to taste, chill, and serve garnished.

Nutritional value per serving:

Calories: 72

Fats: 1g

Carbohydrates: 12g

Salt: 0.43g

Saturated fat: 0g

Fiber: 2.7g

orange, **carrot**, & ginger soup

1 medium onion, finely chopped

3 medium carrots, peeled and finely sliced

1$^1/_3$ cups vegetable broth

2in gingerroot, peeled and finely grated

1$^1/_3$ cups water

zest of $^1/_2$ orange

juice of 1 orange

sea salt and freshly-ground black pepper

chopped chives, to garnish

Place the onion, carrots, and broth in a large saucepan, bring to a boil and simmer for 15 minutes. Gather the grated gingerroot into your hand and squeeze the juice into the soup. Discard the gingerroot fiber. Add the water, orange juice, and rind to the pan, bring back to a boil and simmer for another 10 minutes. Remove the pan from the heat and allow the soup to cool slightly before blending in a food processor or blender until smooth. Reheat and serve garnished with chives.

Nutritional value per serving:

Calories: 89

Fats: 1g

Carbohydrates: 19g

Salt: 0.9g

Saturated fat: 0.1g

Fiber: 4.2g

tomato salad

8-12 tomatoes: use one variety, or a mixture, of
   very ripe red or yellow vine-ripened tomatoes
extra-virgin olive oil
2-4 teaspoons basil leaves or mint leaves
sea salt, freshly-ground pepper and sugar

Dressing
6 tablespoons olive oil or a mixture of olive and
   other oils e.g. sunflower and groundnut
2 tablespoons white wine vinegar
$\frac{1}{2}$ level teaspoon mustard (Dijon or English)
$\frac{1}{2}$ level teaspoon salt
few grinds of black pepper
1 garlic clove, peeled (and mashed if not using
   a blender)
sprig of parsley
1 small scallion
sprig of watercress

First, make the dressing: put all the ingredients into a blender and run at medium speed for about 1 minute, or mix oil and vinegar in a bowl and add mustard, salt, pepper, and garlic. Chop the parsley, scallion and watercress finely and add in. Whisk before serving.

Cut the tomatoes in half or lengthways or into wedges, or simply into $\frac{1}{2}$in thick slices depending on shape and size.

Spread out in a single layer on a large flat plate, season with salt, pepper and a sprinkling of sugar. Sprinkle with dressing. Scatter with torn basil or mint leaves. Toss gently, just to coat the tomatoes. Serve soon either as a first course or as an accompanying salad.

TIP
Tomatoes must be dressed as soon as they are cut to seal in their flavor.

Nutritional value per serving:
Calories: 188
Fats: 18g
Carbohydrates: 6g
Salt: 0.96g
Saturated fat: 2.4g
Fiber: 1.8g

avocado & strawberry salad

1 ripe avocado, halved, pitted, peeled, and cut
   into cubes

6 strawberries, hulled and quartered

2 teaspoons lemon juice

2 teaspoons balsamic vinegar

salt and freshly-ground black pepper

Place the avocado in a bowl with the strawberries. Mix together the lemon juice and vinegar, pour over the salad, and mix gently. Season to taste and serve immediately.

Nutritional value per serving:

Calories: 148

Fats: 14g

Carbohydrates: 5g

Salt: 0.52g

Saturated fat: 1.6g

Fiber: 2.8g

spiced yogurt relish

1 red onion, thinly sliced
1 cucumber, halved, pitted, and thinly sliced
1 teaspoon toasted cumin seeds
bunch of cilantro, roughly chopped (stems
  and all)
2 tomatoes, quartered, pitted, and thinly sliced
1¾ cups plain full-fat runny yogurt
salt and freshly-ground black pepper

Combine the onion and cucumber in a strainer, sprinkle liberally with salt, and set over a bowl for 10 minutes. Rinse thoroughly and pat dry – this should rid the cucumber of some of its water and the onion of some of its strength.

Combine the onion and cucumber with the cumin seeds, cilantro, tomatoes, and yogurt. Stir well and adjust the seasoning (carefully, as there is probably enough salt from the cucumber and onion).

Nutritional value per rounded tablespoon:
Calories: 19
Fats: 0g
Carbohydrates: 3g
Salt: 0.1g
Saturated fat: 0.2g
Fiber: 0.3g

moroccan lemon salad

4 ripe, thin-skinned lemons

2 teaspoons olive oil

2 teaspoons or more harissa, to taste

1 bunch flat-leaf parsley, chopped

Slice the lemons into thin rounds, discarding any pips. Add the rest of the ingredients and mix well.

TIP

You can peel the lemons if you don't like things too bitter.

Nutritional value per serving:

Calories: 40

Fats: 3g

Carbohydrates: 3g

Salt: 0.04g

Saturated fat: 0.02g

Fiber: 0.2g

papaya salad

2 garlic cloves, peeled

3–4 small fresh red or green chiles

20 fine beans, chopped into 2in lengths

6oz fresh papaya, peeled, pitted and cut into
   fine slivers

1 tomato, cut into wedges

2 tablespoons *nam pla* (Thai fish sauce)

1 tablespoon granulated sugar

2 tablespoons lime juice

a selection of fresh firm green vegetables in
   season – eg iceberg lettuce, cucumber, white
   cabbage - to serve

Pound the garlic in a large mortar, then add the chiles and pound again. Add the beans, breaking them up slightly. Now take a spoon and stir in the papaya. Lightly pound together, then stir in the tomato and lightly pound again.

Add the fish sauce, sugar, and lime juice, stirring well, then turn into a serving dish. Serve with fresh raw vegetables – any leaves, such as white cabbage, can be used as a scoop for the spicy mixture.

Nutritional value per serving:

Calories: 51

Fats: 0g

Carbohydrates: 11g

Salt: 1.37g

Saturated fat: 0g

Fiber: 2.1g

raw artichoke salad

4 large artichokes, cleaned as below

1 bunch scallions

2 large tomatoes, peeled, pitted, and roughly
   chopped

3 tablespoons extra-virgin olive oil

juice of 1 lemon or to taste

1 clove of garlic, finely chopped

$\frac{1}{2}$ lemon sliced into thin slices, each slice cut
   into small wedges

3 tablespoons parsley, roughly chopped

salt and freshly-ground black pepper

Prepare the artichokes as shown below.

Combine the rest of the ingredients in a large salad bowl and mix well. Slice the artichoke hearts into thin crescents and immediately coat with the dressing. Decorate with artichoke leaves and serve.

TIP

This salad improves if left to marinate for a few hours. The artichoke hearts will not discolor once they are coated in the dressing.

How to prepare artichoke hearts

Cut the leaves off halfway down the artichoke, exposing the choky heart. Continue to trim off the leaves carefully until you are left with just the heart and the choke. With a sharp knife scrape away the choke. Immediately plunge the peeled artichoke into cold acidulated water (with lemon juice added) as the cut surface blackens very quickly. Do not throw away the leaves, use to decorate the salad.

Nutritional value per serving:

Calories: 155

Fats: 9g

Carbohydrates: 10g

Salt: 0.44g

Saturated fat: 1.2g

Fiber: 1.2g

eggplant, basil, spinach, & chile salad

2 eggplants

large handful of basil leaves

3 tablespoons olive oil

4 tomatoes, sliced

5 1/2 cups baby spinach

1 garlic clove

3/4 cup yogurt

1 red chile, pitted and finely chopped

1 heaped tablespoon pine nuts

juice of 1 lemon

salt and freshly-ground black pepper

good bread, to serve

TIP

This salad is a good source of calcium, folic acid, fiber and Vitamins A, C, and E.

Nutritional value per serving:

Calories: 194

Fats: 14g

Carbohydrates: 11g

Salt: 0.58g

Saturated fat: 2g

Fiber: 5.2g

Preheat a hot broiler and cook the eggplants as shown below. Transfer to a bowl and cover with plastic wrap. If working in batches, make sure to cover the bowl again each time.

Roughly chop the basil leaves and add these to the bowl, together with the olive oil, tomatoes, and spinach leaves. Mash the garlic with 1/2 teaspoon of salt, whisk this into the yogurt, and add the mixture to the eggplant together with the chile. Heat a dry skillet and, when hot, toast the pine nuts until they just begin to color. Add these to the bowl. Toss everything well together, squeeze over the juice of the lemon, and serve with lots of good bread.

How to charbroil eggplants

Slice the eggplants lengthways into 1/2in slices. Heat a ridged broiler pan over a high heat and brush the eggplant slices (not the broiler) with olive oil. Grill for 2-3 minutes on each side until soft and charred.

tabbouleh

$2/3$ cup bulgur (cracked wheat)

6 tablespoons extra-virgin olive oil

juice of 2 organic lemons or more if you need it, freshly squeezed

3 tablespoons parsley, freshly chopped

3 tablespoons mint, freshly chopped

3 tablespoons spring onion, green and white parts, chopped

salt and freshly-ground pepper

To serve

small crisp lettuce leaves (Romaine or iceberg)

6 very ripe firm tomatoes, (a selection of red and yellow looks great), pitted, diced, and sprinkled with a little salt, pepper, and sugar

1 firm crisp cucumber, cut into $1/4$in dice

arugula leaves or flat-leaf parsley

black olives (optional)

Soak the bulgur in cold water for about 30 minutes, drain, and squeeze well to remove any excess water. Stir in the olive oil and some of the lemon juice. Season with salt and pepper and leave aside to absorb the dressing while you chop the parsley, mint, and scallions. Just before serving, mix the herbs with the bulgur, taste, and add more lemon juice if necessary. It should taste fresh and lively.

To serve: arrange on a serving plate surrounded by lettuce leaves and little mounds of well-seasoned tomato and cucumber dice. Garnish with arugula or sprigs of flat-leaf parsley. A few black olives wouldn't go amiss either if you enjoy them. Warm pita or Middle Eastern flatbread is the perfect accompaniment.

Nutritional value per serving:

Calories: 196

Fats: 12g

Carbohydrates: 19g

Salt: 0.37g

Saturated fat: 1.7g

Fiber: 1.6g

spiced bulgur wheat **pilaf**

4 tablespoons olive oil

1 onion, chopped

2$\frac{1}{2}$ cups bulgur wheat (cracked wheat)

1 teaspoon ground cumin

1 teaspoon ground coriander seeds

1 teaspoon turmeric

1 teaspoon ground ginger

1 x 14oz can of chopped tomatoes

salt and pepper

In a large heavy-based saucepan, heat the olive oil and gently sauté the onion in it for 10 minutes, or until softened.

Add the bulgur wheat and continue to cook for a further 2 minutes, stirring frequently. Add the spices and cook for 2 minutes more, or until the spices lose their raw aroma. Add the tomatoes with their liquid and 1$\frac{1}{3}$ cups of water. Bring to a boil. Season, turn down the heat, and simmer for 15 minutes, uncovered. (You may need a little more water towards the end of the cooking.)

Remove from heat and set aside for 10 minutes, covered with a clean dish towel, before serving.

Nutritional value per serving:

Calories: 388

Fats: 9g

Carbohydrates: 68g

Salt: 0.32g

Saturated fat: 1.3g

Fiber: 1g

warm **cous cous** salad with yellow pesto

1 yellow bell pepper, about 7oz in total

4 tablespoons olive oil

2 tablespoons freshly grated Parmesan

1$^1/_4$ cups chicken or vegetable broth

1 tablespoon unsalted butter

1$^1/_2$ cups cous cous

2 tablespoons snipped fresh chives

TIP

You can make the cous cous in advance, and either serve cold or reheat in the oven, or even better, in a microwave. Stir in the yellow pesto just before serving or the cous cous will lose some of its texture.

Nutritional value per serving:

Calories: 224

Fats: 10g

Carbohydrates: 23g

Salt: 0.21g

Saturated fat: 2.8g

Fiber: 0.6g

Broil the bell peppers as shown below. Transfer to a bowl with tongs and cover with plastic wrap, leave to cool, then peel and discard the skins. Roughly chop the bell pepper flesh and place in a food processor or blender and blend to a purée. Add the Parmesan and the remaining olive oil and blend again until smooth. Season to taste.

Place the broth in a saucepan and add the butter, then season to taste and bring to a simmer. Place the cous cous in a large heatproof bowl and then pour over the broth mixture. Cover with plastic wrap or aluminum foil and set aside for 5 minutes, then using a fork fluff up the grains so that they separate. Stir in the yellow bell pepper pesto and spoon into wide-rimmed bowls. Scatter over the chives and serve warm or cold.

How to broil bell peppers

Cut the bell pepper in half and remove the seeds, stalk, and inner membrane. Place the bell pepper, cut side down in the baking tray and drizzle 1 tablespoon oil on top. Place under a hot broiler for about 10 minutes or until the skin is blackened and blistered.

mixed **wholegrain** salad

¹/₄ cup whole wheatgrain, soaked for 12 hours
   and drained, cooked, and cooled

¹/₄ cup pot barley, cooked and cooled

¹/₄ cup buckwheat groats

Dressing

2 teaspoons brown miso

2 teaspoons cider vinegar

2 teaspoons soy sauce

1 teaspoon extra-virgin olive oil

Place the cooked wheatgrains and barley in a bowl. Dry-roast the buckwheat in a saucepan over a medium heat, until it gives off a nutty aroma. Add plenty of water to cover, bring to a boil and simmer for 10-15 minutes until tender. Drain well and add to the other grains.

Mix together the ingredients for the dressing and stir into the grains. Serve at room temperature.

Nutritional value per serving:

Calories: 290

Fats: 3g

Carbohydrates: 62g

Salt: 1.38g

Saturated fat: 0.4g

Fiber: 1.9g

gujerati-style **spinach** with lemon & black pepper

2 tablespoons vegetable oil

1 garlic clove, crushed

1 teaspoon cumin seeds

2$\frac{1}{4}$lb fresh spinach, well washed

juice and rind of 1 lemon

$\frac{1}{2}$ teaspoon sugar

4 tablespoons plain yogurt

$\frac{1}{4}$ teaspoon black peppercorns, coarsely crushed

salt

Heat the vegetable oil in a deep-sided skillet, add the garlic and cumin seeds and fry for 1 minute to release their fragrance. Add the spinach, raise the heat and turn the spinach in the oil with the garlic and cumin. Add the lemon juice and rind, and cook until the spinach has wilted. Stir in the sugar, yogurt, and black pepper and adjust the seasoning. Serve hot.

TIP

This dish is rich in iron, calcium, folic acid, and fibre, as well as Vitamins A, C, and E.

Nutritional value per serving:

Calories: 129

Fats: 8g

Carbohydrates: 6g

Salt: 1.17g

Saturated fat: 1.1g

Fiber: 5.3g

wok-fried shiitake **mushrooms**

1lb shiitake mushrooms

1 tablespoon sesame oil

2in piece fresh gingerroot, peeled and finely
   chopped

1 large red chile, pitted and diced

6 tablespoons soy sauce

$1/4$ cup chopped fresh lemon balm

Wipe the mushrooms with dampened kitchen paper towels if necessary, then trim the stalks and slice.

Heat a wok until searing hot. Add the sesame oil and just as it begins to smoke, tip in the shiitake mushrooms and sauté gently for 1 minute. Add the gingerroot with chile and soy sauce and stir-fry for a couple of minutes until the mushrooms are tender. Scatter over the lemon balm and spoon into a warmed side dish. Serve at once.

Nutritional value per serving:

Calories: 46

Fats: 3g

Carbohydrates: 2g

Salt: 3.61g

Saturated fat: 0.4g

Fiber: 0.1g

braised baby **leeks** with tapenade

½ cup black olives, pitted (good quality)

2 large garlic cloves, finely chopped

2 teaspoons canned anchovy fillets, finely chopped

2 teaspoons sun-dried tomatoes, chopped (preserved in brine)

3 tablespoons olive oil

16-18 baby leeks, trimmed

Place the olives in a food processor or blender with the garlic, anchovies, sun-dried tomatoes, and the olive oil, then blend to a smooth paste. Season to taste and add a little more oil if you think the tapenade is too thick – it should be the consistency of thick heavy cream.

Place the leeks in a saucepan of boiling salted water and cook for 2-4 minutes or until lightly cooked and just tender – the exact cooking time will depend on their size. Drain and quickly refresh in a bowl of ice-cold water, then pat dry with kitchen paper towels and arrange in a warmed serving dish. Drizzle over the tapenade and serve at once.

Nutritional value per serving:

Calories: 131

Fats: 11g

Carbohydrates: 4g

Salt: 1.51g

Saturated fat: 1.5g

Fibre: 3.1g

carrot, parsnip, & cabbage with mustard seed

3 tablespoons sunflower oil

1 tablespoon black mustard seeds

1 chile, pitted and chopped

1¹/₄ cups carrots, coarsely grated

1¹/₄ cups parsnips, coarsely grated

2 cups cabbage, finely shredded against the grain (see below)

2 tablespoons parsley, chopped

2 tablespoons mint, freshly chopped

salt, freshly-ground pepper and sugar

freshly squeezed lemon juice, to taste

Heat the oil in a sauté pan and add the mustard seeds. They will start to pop almost instantly. Add the chopped chile and stir and cook for a minute or so. Add the carrots, parsnips, and cabbage. Toss over a medium heat for 2 or 3 minutes, then add the parsley and mint and toss again. Season with salt, freshly-ground pepper, and a little sugar. Add the lemon juice, taste and correct seasoning. Serve immediately.

How to shred red or white cabbage

Cut the cabbage into quarters and remove the hard center. Turn each slice onto its side and slice thinly lengthways.

Nutritional value per serving:

Calories: 112

Fats: 7g

Carbohydrates: 10g

Salt: 0.21g

Saturated fat: 0.7g

Fiber: 3.9g

okra with tomatoes

1¹/₂lb fresh okra pods

2 tablespoons oil

1 onion, chopped

2 garlic cloves, chopped

3 large tomatoes, chopped

1 chile pepper, pitted and chopped

1 teaspoon sugar

salt

Prepare the okra by trimming the stalks close to the pod. If you don't enjoy their glueyness – though lots of people do – don't hull, just trim off the stems, toss the pods with salt and a little vinegar, and leave in a colander for an hour or two, by which time they will have yielded up their gloop; rinse well before using. Chunk.

Warm the oil in a heavy saucepan or casserole and gently fry the onion and garlic until soft – don't let it brown. Add the tomato, chile, and sugar and bubble up, squashing with a wooden spoon to encourage a rich little sauce. Stir in the okra, add a glass of water, and bubble up. Turn down the heat, put the lid on loosely and simmer for 30 minutes, until the pods are perfectly tender and the sauce deliciously rich and sticky. Or bake in the oven at 300°F. Serve at room temperature, with quartered limes and chili-pepper sauce on the side.

TIP

For a more substantial dish, include slivers of beef or pork tossed in the hot oil when you fry the onion and garlic, or finish with a handful of fresh shrimp.

This dish is a good source of calcium, folic acid, and fiber, as well as Vitamins A and C.

Nutritional value per serving:

Calories: 124

Fats: 7g

Carbohydrates: 11g

Salt: 0.3g

Saturated fat: 0.7g

Fiber: 6.6g

delicious
desserts

strawberries with bitter orange & honey

1$\frac{1}{2}$ cups (about 1lb) big strawberries

4 tablespoons dark forest honey

2 bitter oranges, strips of rind and juice

Hull the strawberries and wipe them, but don't wash. Heat the honey in a small saucepan with the orange juice and rind and simmer for about 10 minutes, until the honey thickens and acquires the flavor of the orange. Dress the strawberries with the honey.

TIP

Lemon juice or sherry vinegar can replace the bitter orange juice.

Nutritional value per serving:

Calories: 83

Fats: 0g

Carbohydrates: 21g

Salt: 0.02g

Saturated fat: 0g

Fiber: 1.3g

four melon & ginger salad

2in piece gingerroot
$1/2$ cup raw brown sugar
$1^1/_4$ cups water
4 small melons eg. Ogen, watermelon,
   cantaloupe, honeydew
large tub Greek yogurt

Shred the gingerroot into a small saucepan. Use a pastry brush dipped in a little of the water to brush down the shredder and release all the bits. Add the sugar and water to the pan and cook slowly to dissolve the sugar. Bring to a boil and simmer fairly fast, keeping a watchful eye on the mixture for 10-15 minutes until it has reduced by half and become thick and syrupy. Pass through a fine strainer and chill.

Cut the melons into sections and remove the skin and seeds. Cut into smaller wedges or slices and arrange a few of each variety on dessert plates or one large platter. Spoon over the ginger syrup and serve with yogurt.

Nutritional value per serving:
Calories: 200
Fats: 6g
Carbohydrates: 32g
Salt: 0.24g
Saturated fat: 3.6g
Fiber: 1.5g

fruit kebabs

8 peaches or nectarines

8 apricots

24 cherries

16 strawberries

4 bananas

fresh lemon juice

orange liqueur (Cointreau or Grand Marnier)

1 cup superfine sugar

whipping cream

Cut the peaches or nectarines and apricots in halves, discarding the pits, and keep the strawberries and cherries whole. Peel the bananas and cut into large chunks about $3/4$in long and sprinkle with a little lemon juice. Mix the fruit in a bowl, sprinkle with orange liqueur, and macerate for about 15 minutes.

Thread the fruit onto skewers. Roll in superfine sugar and barbecue for 5-8 minutes or until they start to caramelize. Serve immediately with a little softly whipped cream. For real excitement, pour some of the liqueur over each, set it alight, and serve immediately. Otherwise just drink the marinade with the kebabs later on!

Nutritional value per kebab:

Calories: 109

Fats: 0g

Carbohydrates: 26g

Salt: 0.01g

Saturated fat: 0g

Fiber: 1.9g

plums baked in red wine & cranberry juice

$^1/_2$ stick unsalted butter

8 plump red plums, halved and pitted

1$^3/_4$ cups mixed red wine and cranberry juice

4 large sprigs mint, finely chopped

4 tablespoons brown superfine sugar

Preheat the oven to 350°F.

Rub the bottom of a shallow casserole dish with half the butter. Sprinkle with half the sugar and lay the plums on top, cut side down. Pour over the wine and cranberry juice, and sprinkle with the mint.

Dot the rest of the butter on top and dust with the remaining sugar.

Bake for 20 minutes.

Nutritional value per serving:

Calories: 252

Fats: 10g

Carbohydrates: 31g

Salt: 0.04g

Saturated fat: 6.5g

Fiber: 1.7g

scented pears

1 bottle full-bodied soft red wine

6 tablespoons lavender or other fragrant honey

2 tablespoons black peppercorns, tied in a
   cheesecloth bag

6 sprigs lavender flowers

juice and rind of 1 lemon

6 ripe pears, peeled, with the stem attached

6 sprigs of lavender flowers and mint to
   decorate

Combine the wine, honey, peppercorns, lavender flowers, and lemon juice and rind in a large, heavy saucepan. Bring to a boil and cook for 2 minutes.

Reduce the heat, add the pears and simmer, very gently, for 10 minutes. Remove from the heat and allow to cool. Serve the pears with a little of the cooking liquid and decorated with the lavender blossom and mint.

Nutritional value per serving:

Calories: 186

Fats: 0g

Carbohydrates: 27g

Salt: 0.04g

Saturated fat: 0g

Fiber: 3.3g

rhubarb phyllo parcels

1¹/₂lb rhubarb

²/₃ cup brown sugar

1 teaspoon chopped gingerroot

¹/₂ stick butter

6 sheets phyllo pastry

²/₃ cup very low-fat cream cheese or Greek
   yogurt

Preheat the oven to 425°F. Butter a large baking sheet. Trim the rhubarb and cut into 1in lengths. Place in a single layer in a large ovenproof dish. Sprinkle over the sugar and the gingerroot. Cover with a piece of aluminum foil and bake for 20 minutes or until the rhubarb is tender and has released its juices. Remove from the oven, cool, and strain. Discard any excess juice.

Melt the butter in a small saucepan. Lay one sheet of phyllo pastry on the work surface and brush it with melted butter. Lay a second sheet on top and brush again. Cut into six 5in squares. Place a heaped teaspoonful of the rhubarb in the center of each square, followed by a teaspoonful of cream cheese. Make into purse shapes as shown below and place on the baking sheet. Bake for 15 minutes until golden brown.

How to make phyllo parcels

Place the filling on the center of each square of phyllo pastry. Take opposite corners and pinch together. Repeat with remaining two corners and twist together well.

Nutritional value per serving:

Calories: 278

Fats: 8g

Carbohydrates: 48g

Salt: 0.89g

Saturated fat: 4.6g

Fiber: 1.5g

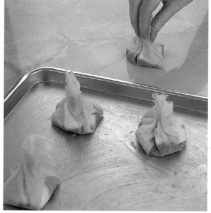

index

Artichokes

Raw Artichoke Salad 136

Asparagus

Chilled Asparagus & Lemon Soup 122

Cornish Crab & Asparagus Salad 44

Avocados

Avocado & Strawberry Salad 128

Chicken Tortillas with Avocado, Chili & Sour Cream 94

Chicken with Peppers, Guacamole, & Chili Oil 60

Chilled Avocado Soup 118

Cornish Crab & Asparagus Salad 44

Seared Scallops with Guacamole, Cilantro & Chile 68

Tomato, Mozzarella, & Avocado salad 30

Baked Mackerel with Carrot Noodles 84

Baked Stuffed Trout 92

Beef & Vegetable Noodles with Black Beans 108

Beetroot

Beetroot, Arugula, Apple, & Cashew Nut Salad 38

Cabbage & Beetroot Soup 114

Braised Baby Leeks with Tapenade 152

Breakfast

Compote of Dried Fruit 20

Fruit-filled Melon Shells 18

Granola 26

Honey, Fruit & Yogurt 22

Oatmeal Porridge 24

Orange & Pineapple Smoothie 14

Strawberry & Raspberry Smoothie 16

Broccoli

Spicy Noodles with Tomatoes 54

Bulgur Wheat

Spiced Bulgur Wheat Pilaf 142

Tabbouleh 140

Cabbage

Cabbage & Beetroot Soup 114

Carrot, Parsnip, & Cabbage with Mustard Seed 154

Cabbage and Beetroot Soup 114

Calves' Liver with Almonds 102

Carrot

Baked Mackerel with Carrot Noodles 84

Carrot, Parsnip, & Cabbage with Mustard Seed 154

Crab & Asparagus Salad 44

Orange, Carrot, & Ginger Soup 124

Stir-fried Vegetables with Shrimp 42

Cheese

Cypriot Salad 36

Tomato, Mozzarella, & Avocado Salad 30

Chicken

Chicken Tortillas with Avocado, Chili & Sour Cream 94

Chicken with Peppers, Guacamole, & Chili Oil 60

Pan-broiled Chicken Breasts with Cardamom 96

Chilled Asparagus & Lemon Soup 122

Chilled Avocado Soup 118

Clams with Chile & Basil 70

Compote of Dried Fruit 20

Cous cous

Spicy Shrimp Cous cous 52

Warm Cous cous Salad with Yellow Pesto 144

Crab & Asparagus Salad 44

Cypriot Salad 36

Egg Noodles with Stir-Fried Vegetables 58

Eggplant

Eggplant, Basil, Spinach, & Chile Salad 138

Squid with Dry Curry 76

Fish

Baked Mackerel with Carrot Noodles 84

Baked Stuffed Trout 92

Fisherman's Clams 72

Grilled Flounder on the Bone 82

Grilled Tuna with Salsa Verde 90

Medallion of Cod with Soy & Choy Sum 80
Mullet in a Parcel 86
Pickled Herring with Potato & Tomato
Salad 32
Salad with Tuna-stuffed Bell Pepper 40
Seared Fillet of Salmon with New Potatoes
& Citrus Salad 78
Steamed Fish with Chili Paste 88
Four Melon & Ginger Salad 162

Fruit
Compote of Dried Fruit 20
Four Melon & Ginger Salad 162
Fruit Kebabs 164
Fruit-filled Melon Shells 18
Honey, Fruit, & Yogurt 22
Lamb Steaks with Fresh Apricot Sauce 104
Lobster & Mango Salad 48
Moroccan Lemon Salad 132
Orange, Carrot, & Ginger Soup 124
Orange & Pineapple Smoothie 16
Papaya Salad 134
Plums Baked in Red Wine & Cranberry
Juice 166
Rhubarb Phyllo Parcels 170
Seared Fillet of Salmon with New Potatoes
& Citrus Salad 78
Scented Pears 168

Strawberry & Raspberry Smoothie 16
Tropical Salad 50
Whole Boneless Quail with Peaches 98
Fruit-filled Melon Shells 18
Granola 26
Green & Red Pasta Salad 56
Grilled Flounder on the Bone 82
Grilled Tuna with Salsa Verde 90
Gujerati-style Spinach with Lemon and Black
Pepper 148
Honey, Fruit & Yogurt 22
Lamb Steaks with Fresh Apricot Sauce 104

Leeks
Braised Baby Leeks with Tapenade 152
Lobster & Mango Salad 48
Marinated Steak Skewers 106

Meat
Beef & Vegetables Noodles with Black
Beans 108
Calves' Liver with Almonds 102
Lamb Steaks with Fresh Apricot
Sauce 104
Marinated Steak Skewers 106
Vietnamese Pork & Lemongrass Patties
100
Medallion of Cod with Soy & Choy Sum 80

Melon

Four Melon & Ginger Salad 162
Fruit-filled Melon Shells 18
Mixed Wholegrain Salad 146
Moroccan Lemon Salad 132
Mullet in a Parcel 86

Mushrooms
Marinated Steak Skewers 106
Wok-fried Shiitake Mushrooms 150
Stir-fried Vegetables with Shrimp 42
Mussel Soup with Fine Beans, Tomato, &
Cilantro 116

Nuts
Calves' Liver with Almonds 102
Beetroot, Arugula, Apple, & Cashew Nut
Salad 38
Oatmeal Porridge 24

Okra
Okra and Bean Stew 110
Okra with Tomatoes 156
Orange, Carrot, & Ginger Soup 124
Orange & Pineapple Smoothie 14
Pan-grilled Chicken Breasts with Cardamom
96
Papaya Salad 134

Pasta
Beef & Vegetable Noodles with Black

Beans 108

Egg Noodles with Stir-Fried Vegetables 58

Green & Red Pasta Salad 56

Spicy Noodles with Tomatoes 54

Peppers

Chicken with Peppers, Guacamole, & Chili Oil 60

Salad with Tuna-Stuffed Bell Pepper 40

Spiced Gazpacho 120

Pickled Herring with Potato & Tomato Salad 32

Plums Baked in Red Wine & Cranberry Juice 166

Potatoes

Pickled Herring with Potato & Tomato Salad 32

Seared Fillet of Salmon with New Potatoes & Citrus Salad 78

Shrimp, Potato, & Basil Salad 34

Raw Artichoke Salad 136

Rhubarb Phyllo Parcels 170

Salads

Avocado & Strawberry Salad 128

Beetroot, Arugula, Apple, & Cashew Nut Salad 38

Cornish Crab & Asparagus Salad 44

Cypriot Salad 36

Eggplant, Basil, Spinach, & Chile Salad 138

Four Melon and Ginger Salad 162

Lobster & Mango Salad 48

Mixed Wholegrain Salad 146

Moroccan Lemon Salad 132

Papaya Salad 134

Salad with Tuna-Stuffed Bell Pepper 40

Seared Fillet of Salmon with New Potatoes & Citrus Salad 78

Shrimp, Potato, and Basil Salad 34

Tomato Salad 126

Tomato, Mozzarella & Avocado Salad 30

Tropical Salad 50

Salad with Tuna-Stuffed Bell Pepper 40

Seafood

Clams with Chile & Basil 70

Crab & Asparagus Salad 44

Lobster & Mango Salad 48

Mussel Soup with Fine Beans, Tomato & Cilantro 116

Scallops with Gingerroot, Scallion & Tamarind 66

Seared Scallops with Guacamole, Cilantro & Chile 68

Shrimp, Potato, & Basil Salad 34

Spiced Indian Crab 46

Spicy Shrimp Couscous 52

Squid with Dry Curry 76

Steamed Citrus Mussels 64

Stir-fried Crab Claws with Scallion, Chili &

Garlic 74

Stir-fried Vegetables with Shrimp 42

Tropical Salad 50

Scallops with Gingerroot, Scallion, & Tamarind 66

Scented Pears 168

Seared Fillet of Salmon with New Potatoes & Citrus Salad 78

Seared Scallops with Guacamole, Cilantro & Chile 68

Shrimp, Potato, & Basil Salad 34

Smoothies

Orange & Pineapple Smoothie 14

Strawberry & Raspberry Smoothie 16

Soups

Cabbage & Beetroot Soup 114

Chilled Asparagus & Lemon Soup 122

Chilled Avocado Soup 118

Mussel Soup with Fine Beans, Tomato & Cilantro 116

Spiced Gazpacho 120

Spiced Bulgur Wheat Pilaf 142

Spiced Gazpacho 120

Spiced Indian Crab 46

Spiced Yogurt Relish 130

Spicy Noodles with Tomatoes 54

Spicy Shrimp Couscous 52

Spinach

Eggplant, Basil, Spinach, & Chile Salad

138
    Green & Red Pasta Salad 56
    Gujerati-style Spinach with Lemon &
    Black Pepper 148
Squid with Dry Curry 76
Steamed Citrus Mussels 64
Steamed Fish with Chili Paste 88
Stir-fried Crab Claws with Scallion, Chili &
    Garlic 74
Stir-fried Vegetables with Shrimp 42
Strawberries
    Avocado & Strawberry Salad 128
    Fruit-filled Melon Shells 18
    Strawberries with Bitter Orange & Honey
    160
    Strawberry & Raspberry Smoothie 16
Tabbouleh 140
Tomatoes
    Mussel Soup with Fine Beans, Tomato &
    Cilantro 116
    Spicy Noodles with Tomatoes 54
    Tomato Salad 126
    Okra with Tomatoes 156
    Pickled Herring with Potato & Tomato
    Salad 32
    Spiced Gazpacho 120
    Tomato, Mozzarella, & Avocado Salad 30
Tropical Salad 50
Vietnamese Pork & Lemongrass Patties 100

Warm Cous cous Salad with Yellow Pesto 144
Whole Boneless Quail with Peaches 98
Wok-fried Shiitake Mushrooms 150
Yogurt
    Eggplant, Basil, Spinach, & Chile Salad
    138
    Honey, Fruit, & Yogurt 22
    Spiced Yogurt Relish 130

acknowledgments

The publishers would like to thank the following authors for permission to use the recipes reproduced on the pages indicated: **Darina Allen:** 24, 26, 48, 54, 82, 96, 100, 126, 140, 154, 164; **Hugo Arnold:** 66, 90, 130, 138, 142; **Ed Baines:** 50; **Aliza Baron-Cohen, Adrian Mercuri and Louisa J Walters:** 14, 16, 34, 36, 38, 64, 120, 122, 124, 128, 146; **Vatcharin Bhumichitr:** 58, 70, 76, 88, 108, 134; **Maddelena Bonino:** 84; **Conrad Gallagher:** 40, 60, 68, 74, 78, 80, 94, 98, 106, 116, 144, 150, 152; **Paul Gayler:** 44, 110, 148; **Elisabeth Luard:** 72, 156, 160; **Alison Price:** 46; **Oded Schwartz:** 86, 104, 132, 136, 168; **Michael van Straten:** 18, 20, 22, 30, 32, 42, 52, 56, 92, 102, 114, 118, 166; **Mandy Wagstaff:** 162, 170.

The publishers would like to thank the following photographers for permission to use the images reproduced on the pages indicated: **Martin Brigdale:** 59, 62, 71, 77, 89, 109, 112, 135; **Julie Dixon:** 87, 105, 133, 137, 169; **Gus Filgate:** 28, 41, 45, 51, 61, 69, 75, 79, 81, 95, 99, 107, 111, 117, 145, 149, 151, 153; **Michelle Garrett:** 85; **Georgia Glynn-Smith:** 1, 9, 158; **Jeremy Hopley:** 47; **Francine Lawrence:** 73, 157, 161; **Ray Main:** 2, 5, 7, 12, 19, 21, 23, 25, 27, 31, 33, 43, 49, 53, 55, 56, 57, 60, 67, 76, 78, 82, 83, 91, 93, 97, 101, 103, 106, 115, 119, 127, 131, 139, 141, 143, 155, 165, 167; **Juliet Piddington:** 15, 17, 35, 37, 39, 65, 121, 123, 125, 129; **Jean-Luc Scotto:** 64, 68, 98, 110, 136, 138, 144, 154, 170; **Sara Taylor:** 163, 171.